HOW TO MAKE PEOPLE WORK FOR YOU, WHILE CALLING YOU A FOOL!

By Bishop O. Innocent.

DEDICATION

To all men of enquiry.

QUOTE

"I believe that we all have a responsibility to give back. No one becomes successful without lots of hard work, support from others, and a little luck. Giving back creates a virtuous cycle that makes everyone more successful."

Ron Conway
Read more at:
https://www.brainyquote.com/topics/hard_work

WHY THIS BOOK

A business man is in it, not just to make profit. He is there to maximize profit!

This can only happen when the workers, partners and other downstream staff are adequately motivated.

In this book, the author teaches how we can motivate the worker or partner by making yourself look stupid in his eye. He shows us how we can make the worker win the bargain and negotiate the contract with a winner takes all attitude that makes him or her feel they own the company or deal!

This book answers the question of what can be done to bring the worker or business partner, who actually lays the golden egg, to be in this much desired, optimal production mood. It draws the lesson from the practical experience of the author who has worked in several settings, including the public and private sectors.

CHAPTER ONE

WHY SHOULD PEOPLE WORK FOR YOU?

They say what makes an ocean great, is not the alluvial deposits it has but the number of small rivers pouring water into it.

If you want to be great, you do not depend on what you can do on your own as an individual but what a large number of people can do for you at the same time. They say it is by far better to have a hundred people giving you one percent of their effort than for you alone to give yourself a hundred percent of your effort. In simple language, a tree cannot make a forest.

The dream may be yours but you need to people the vision. The more the merrier.

I saw something in the Bible I want to bring to your notice. Samson with all his physical strength and his vision to dominate the Philistines, ended up neither king of Philistines nor king of Israel, despite all he could do with his physical strength.

In contrast, David was a man of little physique. But the Bible tells me in 1 Chronicle 12:32 that day by day, there came to David, *to help him, a large number of people until they became equal to the number helping God!* It is noteworthy that David ended up as the king of Israel and his Israel dominated Philistine!

You need people to work out your vision and take it from the drawing board to good success.

If you take a close look at the Fortune 500 companies, they are dominated by companies and ventures employing a large number of people. They may start with one man or one man's idea or invention but certainly get to employ a large number of people who work on the project.

Even the so-called sole traders do not work alone. They employ sales men and bookkeepers as well as security men and body guards that follow them on sales trails.

The more well trained and motivated people you have working for you, the quicker and easier it is to transform from nothing to something noteworthy.

QUOTE

Nope, I don't enjoy work generally.

 Not because I'm lazy;

it's just all so stressful and worrying.

 Rowan Atkinson
Read more at:
https://www.brainyquote.com/topics/lazy

CHAPTER TWO

WHAT YOU NEED TO UNDERSTAND ABOUT HUMAN BEINGS

Most human beings detest hard work. Take it or leave it but you cannot change the fact that those in robotics are looking forward to great harvest. Why is this so? Man is urgently looking for what can reduce his or her labor so that he can have more time for leisure! Go and ask the manufacturers of dish and clothes washers – they will tell you that since the time they hit the market, sales have been in volumes and still counting! The merchants of artificial intelligence are smiling to the bank because many of us are finding it increasingly difficult to even pause and do a little thinking. So if there is a machine to do all the calculations and thinking for us, whoever bothers to add anything without calculators these days?

Let me hit the nail on the earth. Man does not like work for the sake of work. If somebody comes to you and says that he needs a job, what he is actually saying is that he needs money! Why would somebody whose compound is over-grown with weed, dress up and hit the street in search of work? Why would a person whose compound is full of clutter head to the council in search of street cleaning job when they can stay at home and work on their dirty compound?

They are not looking for job. They are looking for what they can do to earn some money. You can call it and income or whatever you like but the truth is that the job is not an end but a means to an end.

QUOTE

For the scripture saith, Thou shalt not muzzle the ox that treadeth out the corn. And, the labourer *is* worthy of his reward.

1 TIMOTHY 5:18 [KJV]

CHAPTER THREE

HERE IS ANOTHER PAINFUL FACT

Everyone is looking for where they will work like an ant but eat like an elephant. It is very hard to see a person who wants to work like an elephant and eat like an ant.

When you meet an army of unemployed people, they are all looking for white collar jobs in air-conditioned offices. They do not want anything to do with sweat and fatigue.

But that is not even the painful thing.

The painful thing is that they all want to work for well established companies. Very few want to risk it with a rising entrepreneur. When we are out to be hired, we only work where we think our effort will yield the highest income possible. Very few consider anything else. We here agents to get us the best bargains because we do not want to put in our best for less pay. If in doubt, ask footballers and other sportsmen. They look out for lucrative contracts and nothing else. Very few say, oh we know Mohammed Ali. Let us go and work for him because he is a man of integrity or because he has made his mark in the sport.

No, instead, we go for the highest bidder.

And here is another stark reality: if the contract can be worded in a way that we actually are better off than the employer, we are quite happier with that. The more the contract is tilted in our favor, the more we like it. THE MORE THE CONTRACT MAKES THE EMPLOYER LOOK STUPID, THE HAPPIER WE ARE.

That is man for you. We do not want to be cheated but we are very willing to take it all to ourselves.

QUOTE

Start with good people, lay out the rules, communicate with your employees, motivate them and reward them. If you do all those things effectively, you can't miss.

 Lee Iacocca
Read more at:
https://www.brainyquote.com/quotes/lee_iacocca_400645

CHAPTER FOUR

SO WHY NOT CASH IN ON THIS REALITY TO GET PEOPLE TO WORK FOR YOU?

Listen to this real life story. In 1987, I was a Lagos based journalist on a small salary. Then a newsmagazine opened in the northern part of Nigeria, where due to constant religious riots and fanaticism, very few Lagos pressmen wanted to go. The northern news media doubled my salary, gave me a chauffeur driven car, free three square meals a day, furnished flat, paid holidays and personal assistants where I had none!

The offer was too tempting for me to reject.

I went because I felt my employers were foolish. What was I to offer to warrant such a contract? Yet I had the offer in writing. So I rushed where angels feared to thread!

Exactly two years hence, there was a religious riot and I ran! To say the least, I lost everything I had saved to the rioters but that is not the striking thing to remember here.

In between that job and the next, I had time to reflect. Why did I go over there?

I received a package that made me think my employer must have been a fool!

Yet, on reflection, I could see that I was the fool. I put in my very best to justify the huge pay and comfort the company was giving me. I must have felt like soccer stars with their weekly jumbo pays. I guess that is the reason you see them picking avoidable injuries sometimes in their desperation to give their best at all times!

On that particular job I risked my life a number of times. I remember a day I was asked to leave at noon and drive a thousand four hundred kilometers from Katsina to Lagos, get a forty-eight page magazine printed and return to Katsina before Durbar started by 9am the next day. The incentive was that I would get a fourteenth month salary as bonus!

We must have driven over the bad roads like car racers, arriving Lagos at about midnight. The road was full of potholes and thieves but we plodded through, myself and the chauffer. Using two Kord printing machines at ago, we were able the magazine ready in two hours.

With the promised incentive in sight, we drove back and reached just as the Durbar horse riders were dashing into the stadium!

Of course, we got the promised fourteenth month salary of the year!

When I returned to Lagos after the religious riot, I had time to reflect and I saw that while thinking my employer was stupid with his offer, I was actually the fool! I was making over a thousand times more money for him than he was actually paying me!

CHAPTER FIVE

LET ME TELL YOU ANOTHER REAL LIFE STORY

I did not stay long on the job market before Zoe Ministries World-wide made me another stupendous offer. Then the ministries had over a thousand branches with the largest one having over ten thousand worshippers. I was asked to publish a magazine aimed at reaching Africa as a whole with news and current affairs while having a center pull out filled with religious news.

They asked me to fix my own pay! And recruit all the staff I needed and on my own terms and conditions. They out-paced the northern employers in every department.

Can you imagine that! I am telling you what is real. The President of Zoe Ministries is still alive with branches in UK and USA among other nations!

I was on that job for four years before I put in a voluntary resignation.

Why did I resign?

First, let me tell you that for each of those four years, the ministry doubled my salary! And in addition, I was given several mouth-watering incentives, including all expenses paid travelling opportunities.

In return, I worked like a fool. I was so enmeshed in the job that I did not have time for my family. One day, my newly-wed wife asked whether my President knew at all that I was newly married! I threw myself into the job, working on it as if my life depended on it. We met our bed times and deadlines. Our financial goals were exceeded and everyone was happy including my employers.

CHAPTER SIX

SO WHAT HAS THAT GOT TO DO WITH ANYTHING?

I learnt an important lesson in life that has helped me to excel in all I do in life today and which I am now sharing with you in this little book.

I discovered that be it a partnership or employer-employee relationship, if you allow the workers to feel you are a fool, they will work for you. Make them offers they cannot resist. Make them more comfortable than kings and they will work more than kings!

Is that not the same reason why soccer stars play club football three times a week and still smile on the job? Is that not why professionals always hire first class agents to hire contracts for them? In the end, they get a nice contract that makes both they and their agents feel that they have a better deal than the employer. So they go to work for the employer.

I even see it on amazon.com. Jeff Bezos and his team make us a win-win offer we cannot resist. They say write readable good books for us: for that, we pay you as much as 70% of whatever the customer pays. They even ask us the writers and authors to fix the price ourselves! Now, I am not a mathematician but it looks to me that 70-30 ratio looks like cheating to the publisher considering the costs the latter has to bear!

Most of us writers know what it cost us to get our books published the traditional way and that when we get as little as ten percent as loyalty from the traditional publisher, it is celebration time. We know that when we, on the other hand, self-publish the traditional way, we have lots of bills to pay. Huge marketing costs stare us in the face as well as much energy to be burnt in the course of promotions.

Little wonder that online publishing has gone online. Consider that Amazon.com is not the only online company. I publish for free on Amazon.

Consider the fact that Partridge charged me a huge some just to mount my book for me on their stand!

Amazon's offer looks stupid but is it?

Because of this offer, many offers have decamped from other publishers, to offer their services to Amazon. Best-selling books are being written for and mounted exclusively for Amazon.com!

So what is the heart of the matter? Are you an employer of labor or a partner somewhere? Why not give your worker or partner such an offer that looks stupid but motivates him or her into working hardest and most intelligently with a view to maximizing his or her profits or gains? Why not allow yourself to be cheated, if that will allow the worker or partner to put in his or her very best?

CHAPTER SEVEN

NOW LET ME TELL YOU WHAT HAPPENS WHEN YOU ALLOW THE WORKER OR PARTNER TO THINK THAT YOU ARE A FOOL

1. **Your employee becomes well motivated to work harder.** He believes that he has defeated you in a negotiation and that he is getting the very best he can get elsewhere, if not better.

2. **He might even think that you are working for him.** Since he appears to get the better deal, he has good reason to believe that you are the one working for him instead of the other way round. For every book

published on Amazon, the company has its share not matter how little.

3. **Other workers and potential workers hear about your generous conditions and aspire to work for you.** This creates a pool of workers or applicants from which you can choose nothing but the very best.

4. **There is a competition among the workers that is in your interest** as it inspires them to each put in their very best at any time.

5. **The workers seek to improve their skills so as to earn more.** This in itself plays to your benefit because they own the song while you own the label and whatever they sing, you get your cut.

6. **They also come up with new ideas.** To be ahead of other workers or executive partners, they do a lot of research and brain storming with their assistants, coaches and advisers with a view to coming up with new products. And all that works for the good of you the employer.

7. **They develop a sense of belonging and buy into the business.** When people feel that they are part owners of any business, they tend to work better than slaves who need the cane to put in extra efforts.

8. **Your profits definitely increase.** There is reduced cost of production and better efficiency as the workers seek better ways to increase their income both of which lead to more earnings for both parties.

9. **It generates positive good will for you with your internal public and this will definitely resonate with the external public in the long run.** When the people inside are happy and speak well of the organization, it invariably rubs off on the external public.

10. **It leads to greater impact on the society and the environment.**

CHAPTER EIGHT

IN SUMMARY, HERE ARE TEN THINGS YOU CAN DO TO MAKE THE WORKER WORK FOR YOU WHILE FEELING THAT YOU ARE EITHER FOOLISH OR SLEEPING WHEN THE CONTRACT WAS SIGNED

1. **GIVE HIM A MOUTH-WATERING, WIN-WIN CONTRACT HE CANNOT RESIST**. Fear not: he or she is going to work out the money from which you will pay or

settle him. Employers of football stars do that every day!

2. **MAKE HIM AS COMFORTABLE AS YOU CAN.** Get his decent and well-furnished and appointed quarters! If possible, get him to visit where you are staying so that he can see that his own apartment might even be better than your own. Do not worry. He is just an employee and one day, his contract will expire and he leaves, leaving the company behind for you.

3. **IF YOU CAN, PAY HIM BETTER THAN THE PRESIDENT OF YOUR COUNTRY.** Let him take a bigger piece of the cake you are baking. It will make him feel that he is the owner of the company but you know quite well that the certificate of the shares are in your hand.

4. **CREATE A NICE WORK ENVIRONMENT THAT PROMOTES PRODUCTIVITY.** If it is possible, allow him work from home and at his own home. Never attempt to micro-manage him. Make him feel as if he is his own boss. Learn from the

government how to allow the businesses to thrive on their own and still pay the corporate taxes voluntarily!

5. **AUTOMATE HIS OFFICE AS MUCH AS POSSIBLE.** This encourages him to produce more since he has to use limited energy for a great out-put using the machines. Give him both internet and intranet. Make sure he has all his energy needs supplied.

6. **SUPPLY HIS BOARD.** Let the best food be available to him. Ask horse trainers – the better you feed a horse, the more the mileage you get from it. Do not worry about the cost of the food. His increased productivity will compensate for it.

7. **GET HIM THE BEST DOCTORS –** remember that a sick cannery does not sing. Neither do malaria struck dolphins summersault! It takes a healthy lion to perform in circuses and unless the lion performs, the spectators do not stand to watch and neither do they part with their money.

8. **LET HIM TRAVEL FIRST CLASS** – he needs to arrive happy for meetings and keep his appointments in great comfort.

9. **DO NOT AIM AT A GREAT PROFIT.** Take just one percent from one worker. Give him ninety-nine percent. Why not allow yourself to be cheated in the short run?

10. **INCREASE THE NUMBER OF WORKERS** – our ancestors were very right when they advised that we do not put all our eggs in one basket. No horse racer ever puts all his hope in one horse, no matter how strong or good the horse may be. Get a large number of rivers flowing into your ocean! Look for ninety-nine other workers who can give him the same one percent! They have said it that it is better to have a hundred workers who can give you just one percent each as opposed to you doing all the job by yourself and giving yourself hundred percent! You might even break down in the process and the entire hundred percent from you goes to one lucky doctor somewhere!

When 7up Bottling Company first promised to give out Racer Daewoo cars in Nigeria to those who can find the image in the bottle caps, then twelve million per car was a lot of money in the country and I went to see the Purchasing Manager of the time and to whom I had access.

He told me that I was worried for nothing. He said that the company was not getting the money from one bottle of mineral water sold! Rather, as he told me, the company was selling one billion bottles per year!

Now the promo was once a year. He made me see that even if the company made only one naira per bottle, it would be making one billion naira! So what was one hundred and forty-four million naira that it would not be able to give out?

THE STRIKING FACT IS THIS: THE COMPANY WAS NOT RELYING ON

ONE BOTTLE. IT SPREAD ITS RISKS ON ONE BILLION BOTTLES!

Let us keep in mind that the more the merrier and that we must not rely on one worker. The more the number of goose laying the golden egg, the better for the owner of the company! It is by far better to take a small percentage from a number of happy workforce than a large chunk from an individual worker.

So why not allow them to cheat you by providing them all they need to produce and getting good pay that eats deep into your profit but which you scoop back over a large spread of workers?

OTHER BOOKS BY THE SAME AUTHOR

1. FOURTEEN SIMPLE THINGS YOUR CAN DO TO PROTECT YOURSELF AGAINST TERRORISM

2. SEVEN SIMPLE WAYS TO KNOW A FAKE PASTOR

3. ONE HUNDRED AND TEN PRAYER POINTS FOR A MARRIED WOMAN

4. PARENTING AN ADULT: 25 POSITIONS YOU MUST NEVER ACCEPT IN LIFE

5. APOSTASY; HOW ONE CAN FALL INTO IT WITHOUT KNOWING

6. TWENTY-ONE IRREFUTALBE WAYS PASTORS EXPOSE THEMSELVES TO SEXUAL IMMORALITY

YOU MADE A WISE DECISION!

What makes us so confident in making the above assertion?

It is certainly not because the author:

BISHOP O. INNOCENT

is the president of a seminary and a pastor of many years standing. No!

One word from God through this book is enough to lift your destiny!

Remember that God spoke through a Donkey in the Bible. He can use anyone or book to speak to you.

May the Lord bring this to pass in your life, in Jesus name, we pray!

THANK YOU

- For making out time to read this book. The author will appreciate your honest comments for the improvement of this book in subsequent editions.

For that purpose, kindly contact the author on:

Email: newochei@gmail.com

Thanks and God bless you.

NOTES

NOTES

NOTES

NOTES

NOTES

ABOUT THE AUTHOR

Bishop O. Innocent has worked in various public and private organizations, for over forty-three years now. He began with government ministries and later as a private sector staff of a multi-national company amongst others.

Today, he is self-employed in part-time business.

He holds qualifications in management, consultancy, theology and contemporary Christian ministry.

He uses his skills as a practicing as a journalist to share his findings on the subject with ease.

He is married with grown up children and is currently a seminary president.